The International Design Library®

SOUTHEASTERN WOODLAND INDIAN DESIGNS

Caren Caraway

Stemmer House
PUBLISHERS, INC.
Owings Mills, Maryland

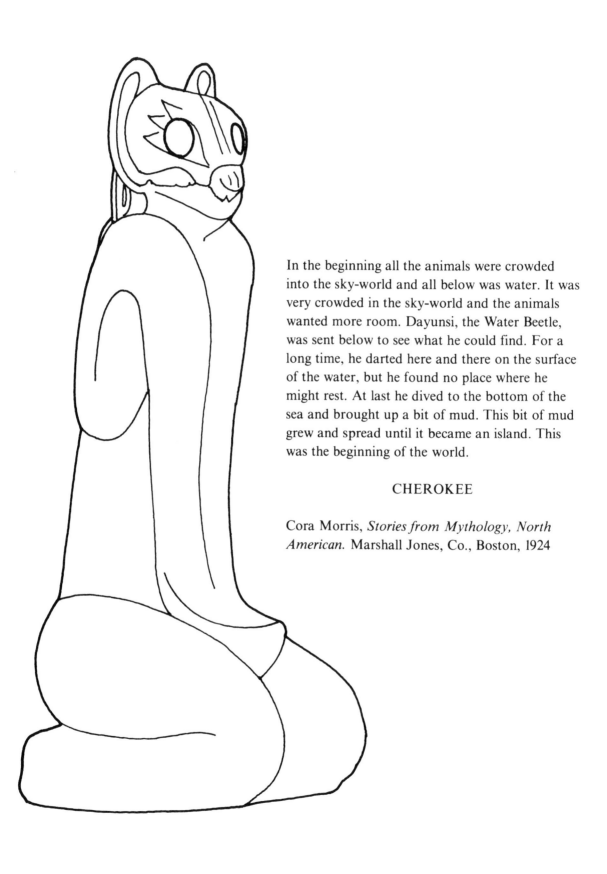

In the beginning all the animals were crowded into the sky-world and all below was water. It was very crowded in the sky-world and the animals wanted more room. Dayunsi, the Water Beetle, was sent below to see what he could find. For a long time, he darted here and there on the surface of the water, but he found no place where he might rest. At last he dived to the bottom of the sea and brought up a bit of mud. This bit of mud grew and spread until it became an island. This was the beginning of the world.

CHEROKEE

Cora Morris, *Stories from Mythology, North American.* Marshall Jones, Co., Boston, 1924

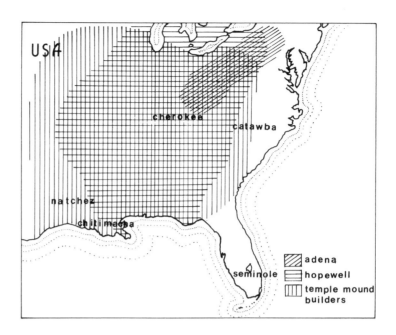

Introduction

THE DECIDUOUS WOODLANDS OF THE SOUTHEASTERN United States that extend from Texas to the Atlantic Ocean have not only been an environment for abundant varieties of flora and fauna. In prehistoric times they were the setting for the most highly developed civilizations north of Mexico.

The ADENA moved into the Ohio Valley 3,000 years ago and founded a culture that lasted for fifteen centuries. The people were tall and powerfully built. Men were nearly seven feet tall and many women were over six feet. They fished, hunted wild animals, ate snails and freshwater mussels, and gathered chestnut, pawpaw, walnuts and raspberries. They may have cultivated squash, pumpkins and sunflowers. Their circular houses of lashed-post walls and thatched roofs were clustered in small villages. Large fields were often enclosed by high, narrow ridges of earth. With elaborate ceremony they buried their dead, some in many layers, along with abundant art works, in gigantic funeral mounds.

The HOPEWELL forced their way into Adena territory 2400 years ago. They developed a vast, powerful civilization based on a loose confederation of tribes led by an elite upper class. Their economy was based on gathering wild foods, hunting, fishing and farming, for they planted corn and beans in small gardens. But their culture influenced the area from northern Wisconsin to the Gulf of Mexico, from the Kansas plains to the Atlantic Ocean. Traveling along rivers in oak log canoes, the Hopewell established a trade network that covered two-thirds of the United States. Using materials gathered from across that vast region, Hopewell artists, the greatest of prehistoric Indians, created an abundance of art works. Copper from Lake Superior tribes was made into knives, axes, headdresses, breastplates, bracelets, rings, ear ornaments, and figures of birds, animals and humans. Delicate silhouettes were carved of mica from Appalachia. Beads and necklaces were fashioned from conch shells, barracuda jaws and alligator teeth from the Gulf of Mexico. Ornaments and cups were

manufactured from sea shells from the Atlantic Coast. Spearheads were chipped from obsidian from Yellowstone. The Hopewell also made beautifully decorated pottery; finely woven mats; clothing of furs, tanned skins and fabric woven from tree bark and plant stems; and stone pipes in the form of birds and animals. They made beads from freshwater pearls, shell and iron, and ear decorations and necklaces from grizzly bear teeth and pearls. They created tools of stone, bone, wood and copper, and exquisitely carved figures of bone, wood and metal. The Hopewell were the finest metalworkers of their time and they constructed ornaments of copper, gold and silver. They built enormous embankments, huge geometric earthworks and wide avenues. They buried their dead in thousands of burial mounds. The corpses were enveloped from head to feet in thousands of pearls and beads and pounds of copper sheets and nuggets. They were surrounded by sculpture and pottery, then covered with tons of earth. After about 500 AD the spectacular funeral practices declined as did the trade in materials from which fine articles had been made. The culture disappeared 1500 years ago for unknown reasons.

Two centuries or so after the decline of the Hopewells, the TEMPLE MOUND BUILDERS created a prosperous and sophisticated culture that corn made possible. After 700 AD the civilization spread throughout the Southeast and the Midwest. It had many similarities with the cultures of Mexico, such as sun-god worship, belief in the feathered serpent, the structure of town life, pottery designs, cultivation of corn varieties, and the construction of great mounds. Mounds were built for temples, tombs and residences of nobles. There were great pyramids 100 feet tall, 700 feet wide and 1000 feet long. There were also huge ceremonial sites that were religious and trading centers for the widespread trade made accessible by river travel. The nobility had splendid houses. They wore feather capes, necklaces, earrings, and leg arm bands of pearls, shells and copper. They painted their faces and had elaborately coiffed hair topped with ornate headdresses. They had servants, who may have been killed to serve them even in death. Many corpses have been found with their hands and heads cut off. The apex of the culture was reached about 1200 AD when the Buzzard or Southern cult flourished. Craftsman were expert in many decorative techniques and used a wide variety of materials, including stone, shell and clay. Some artifacts had cult symbols which indicated violence and death. The culture had vanished by the time of the European's arrival, except for the Natchez.

The NATCHEZ was a culture in which corn cultivation was the major economic activity, although beans, pumpkins and smoking tobacco were also raised. Households consisted of extended families. Aristocrats had to choose their mates from the commoners, but their children had the rank of nobility. A man had lifelong control of his children. Boys were taught to hunt, conduct war and help cultivate crops. Girls learned to cook meals, make clothes and plant crops. There were few sexual inhibitions after puberty, but a girl was expected to charge for her favors in order to build up a dowry. The Natchez were ruled absolutely by a living deity, the Great Sun, who lived on the highest pyramid mound in the tribe's primary village. This deity was aided by his mother, "White Woman," his brothers and sisters and other female relatives. The Great Sun had life-and-death power. At his own death, many followers were drugged and publicly strangled.

The other Indians of the Southeast Woodlands probably comprised 150 to 200 separate groups. Although there was a wide variety of languages, there were some common beliefs, olan systems and matrilineal families. The universe was believed to consist of three separate but related Worlds: Upper, Lower and This World. This World, where man, most animals and all plants live, is a round island resting on the surface of waters. In the universe opposites are constantly at war, and This World hovers between the perfection of the Upper World and the chaos of the Lower World. Man has to find a balance between the two worlds. Herbs were one of the good forces the Indians used to balance evil. They were extremely knowledgeable in herbal medicine. Tobacco was thought to be the most important plant, with the power to bring good or bad fortune, heal or hurt, and influence good and evil spirits.

People were organized into clans named for animals. Clan membership was determined by blood ties related matrilineally. Clan loyalty dominated life. Exact revenge was sought for any transgression from a slight hurt to murder. War was fought by twenty to forty volunteers who painted themselves red and black and fought with clubs, lances, bows and arrows, darts, pikes and slings. The battles were brief and the casualties were usually few. Victors scalped their slain victims. Some captives were adopted or made into slaves. Others were killed by such torture as being scalped alive, during which time they were expected to sing a death-song until they lost consciousness. Achievements in war determined a man's place in society, as did religion and healing. The titular village head was chosen by community leaders, and led by example and persuasion rather than force. The community council of men also discussed items of concern, such as building and repair of public buildings and barricades, planting, etc. Villages were usually laid out around a central plaza and many were surrounded by palisades. There was a public building for winter council meetings and three or four

open sheds for summer meetings. There was a pole in the plaza for poleball games and two or three poles for the display of captives and scalps.

Houses sheltered several different families from a single clan. Marriage between a man and woman of the same clan was prohibited. Marriages were arranged by older women, after which the girl was asked for her consent. Sex before marriage was allowed, but before the couple could live together the boy had to prove his manhood by building a dwelling, then killing a bear or deer for food. He presented some of the meat to the girl, who gave him an ear of corn or food she had cooked. This was considered to be the wedding ceremony for a trial marriage. They lived in the house the boy had built, but either was free to leave. If the relationship dissolved within a year the house belonged to the girl. Otherwise the marriage was considered firm at the end of a year. With the wife's consent, the man could take a second or third wife, often a sister of the first wife. Before marriage a girl could have affairs, but after marriage she was sometimes punished for adultery by having her ears cut off and her marriage dissolved. In some tribes a widow was expected to mourn for four years before remarriage. A woman lived apart from the community during menstruation. Pregnant women avoided certain foods thought to cause birthmarks or a difficult birth. A newborn child was immediately dipped in a creek or river in summer or rolled in snow in winter. It was then rubbed all over with bear grease and tightly bound to a cradleboard where it spent the first year of its life. Most tribes bound the skull to flatten it in back, to enhance its beauty and improve eye sight. Girls learned housework, gardening, pottery-making, basketry and fire-tending. Boys were taught to be hunters and warriors. After proving himself in battle by killing or maiming, a boy was accepted as a man and took his place in the council with a new name, and was granted a war title that recalled his martial feats. There was a great celebration when titles and names were awarded. An even more important celebration was Busk or the Green Corn Ceremony. It was the most sacred holiday, marking the ending of the old and beginning of the new year. The Southeast Indians made a great variety of fine ceramic bowls, bottles, urns and dishes. They fashioned feather capes, beaded belts, bags and shoulder sashes and some of the most complex yarn sashes ever found. Baskets were made of split and plaited cane. Destroyed after the arrival of the white man, creation of this artwork ceased, by and large.

In 1513 Juan Ponce de Leon landed in Florida. The Spaniards, first of the Europeans, pillaged, burned, killed and enslaved the native Americans. Entire tribes were decimated by foreign diseases. The decline which had begun long before the arrival of the Europeans was accelerated. Essentially, the traditional way of life of the Southeast Woodland Indians ended as entire tribes became extinct and others adopted the ways of the white man. The "Five Civilized Tribes," Cherokee, Creek, Chickasaw, Choctaw and Seminole, organized their own universities and newspapers, aided by the invention of the Cherokee alphabet in 1821. In 1830 the Five Tribes moved to Oklahoma, leaving only scattered groups in the Southeast.

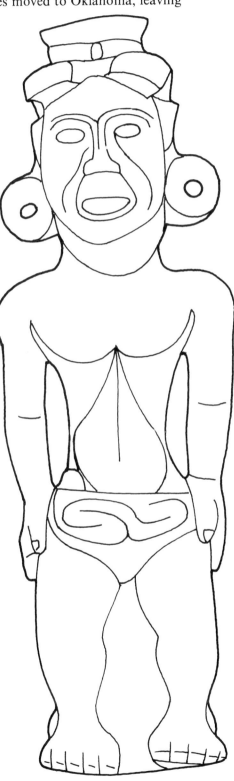

The SEMINOLES, loose groupings of people sharing a common culture, and descendants of the Creek, fled in the eighteenth century from British-dominated Georgia and Alabama to Spanish-controlled Florida. In 1817 Andrew Jackson — and later others — pillaged the Seminoles, who fled to the edges of the swamps. After a bloody guerilla war, most Seminoles were sent to Indian Territory in the west, but a remnant stayed in the Everglades. Today there are four reservations, where they retain much of their distinct traditional identity. They live in houses built on platforms above the swamp. Marriage is casual, and divorce occurs when the husband leaves the house. After the introduction of cotton cloth in the mid-nineteenth century and the acquisition of hand-cranked sewing machines at the beginning of the twentieth century, the Seminoles began to create beautiful, colorful patchwork cloth for their clothing, and this became a traditional art form. The Chitimacha continue to make fine basketry, the Cherokee and Catawba make pottery and the Cherokee make wooden masks and figures, blow guns and split baskets for tourists.

C.C.

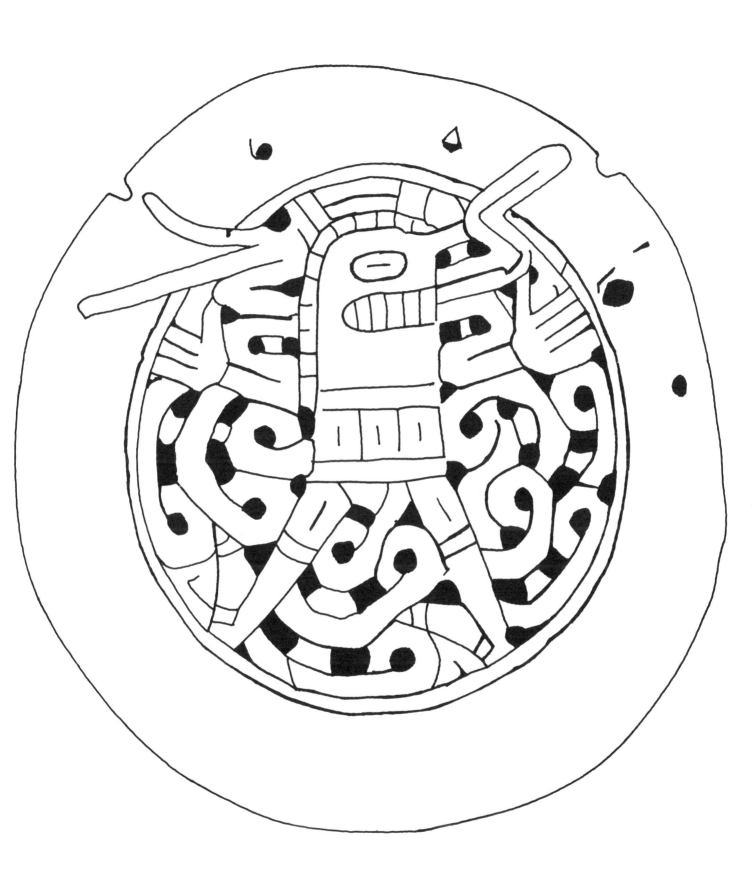

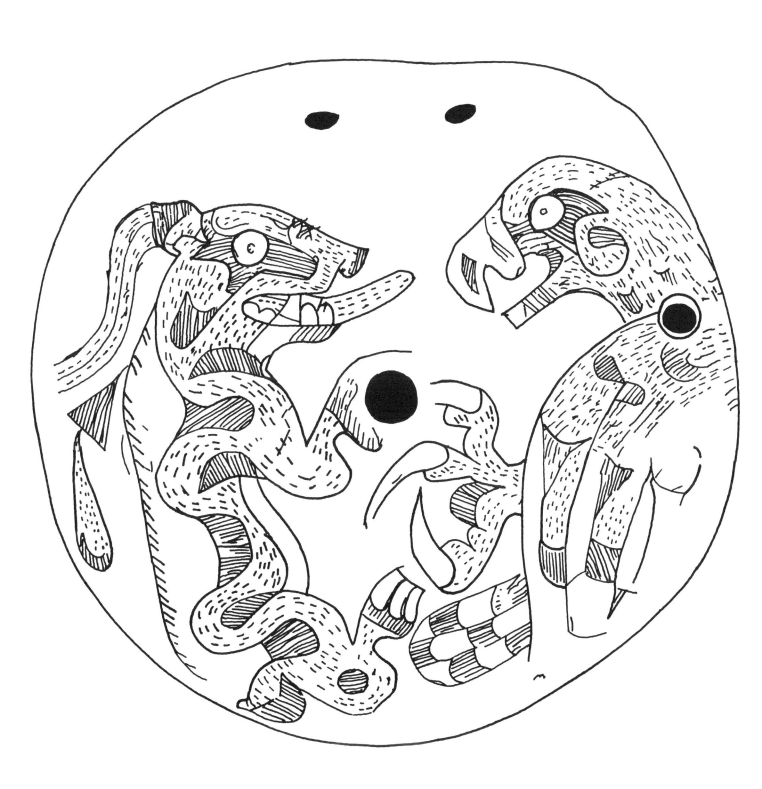

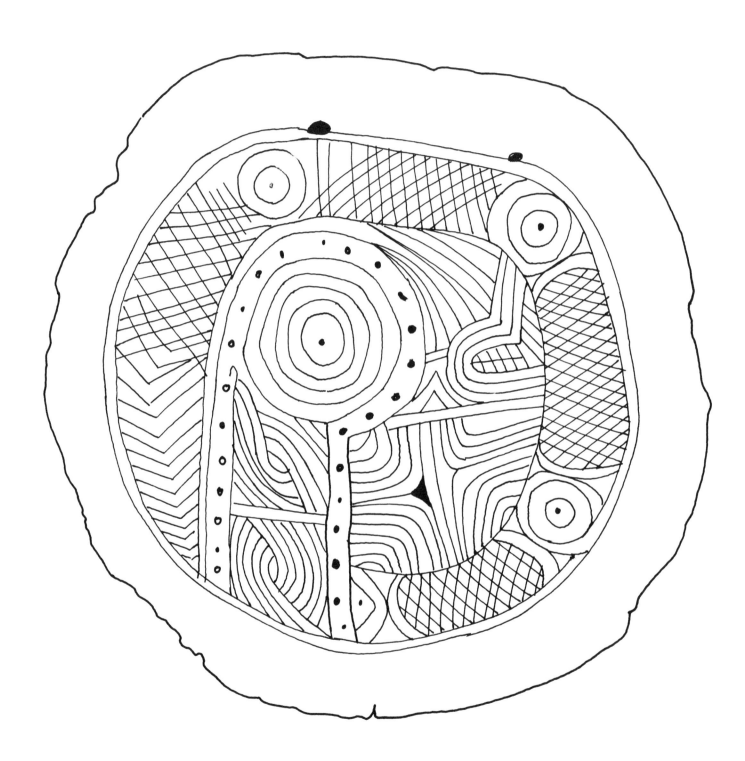

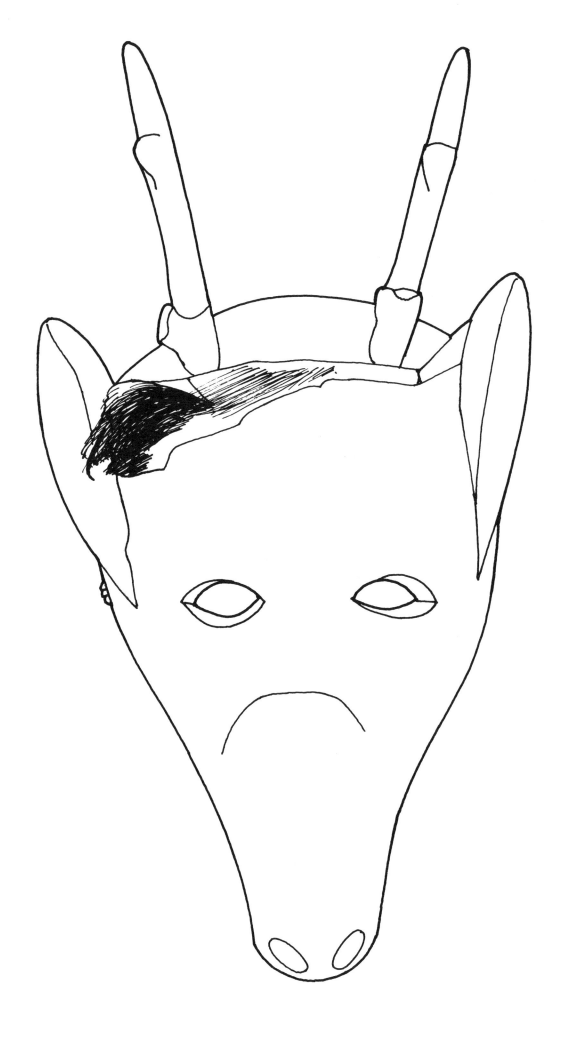

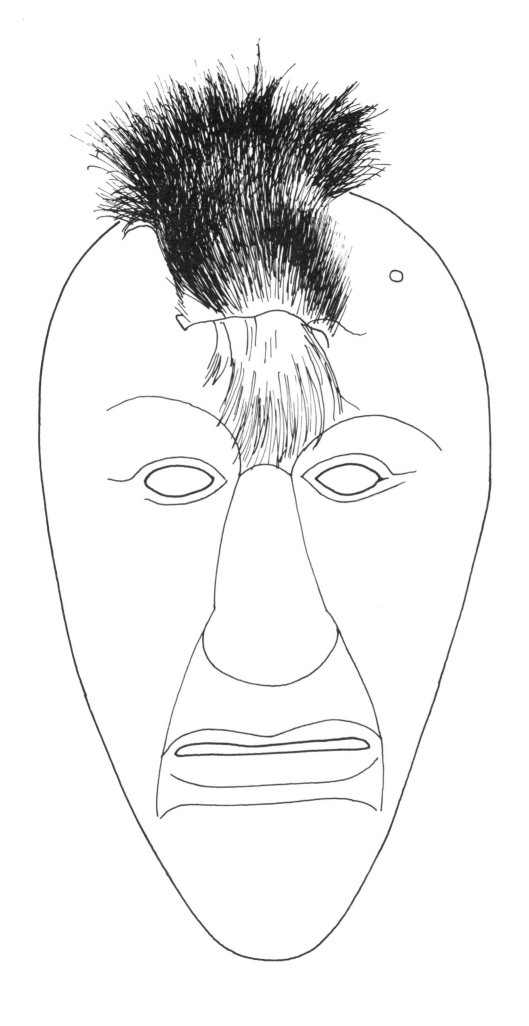

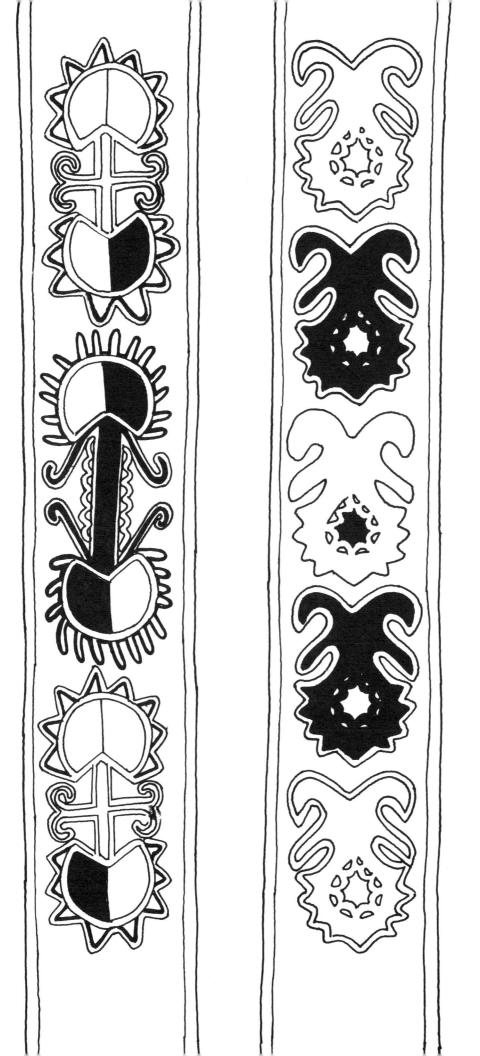

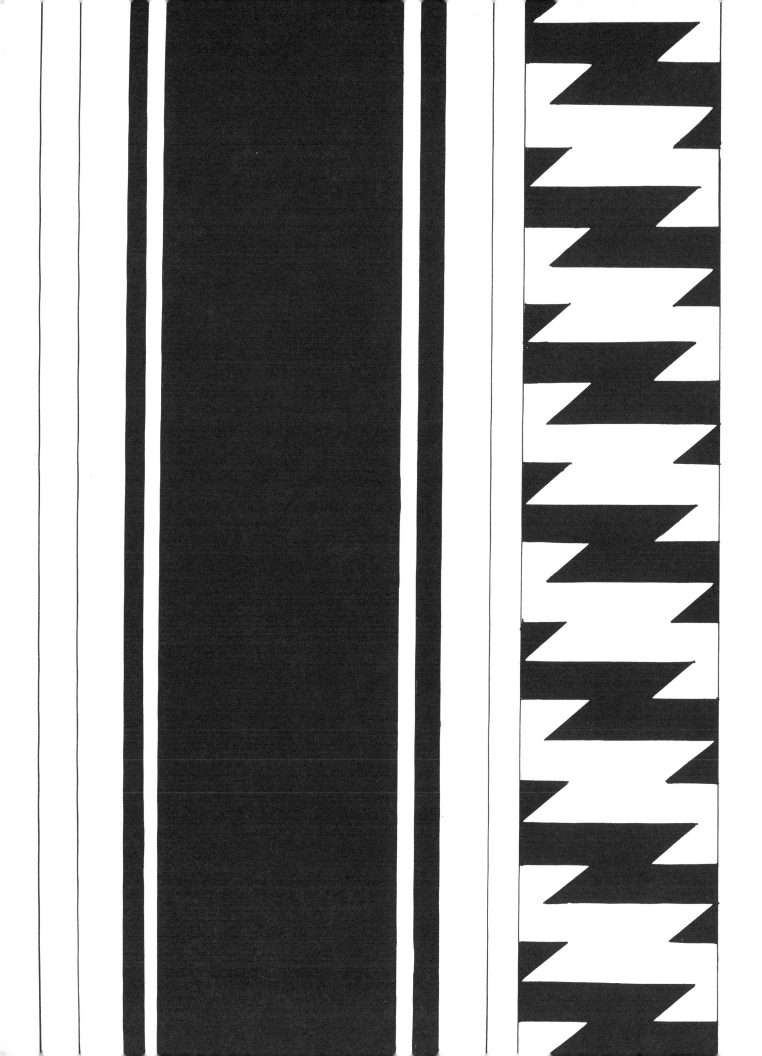

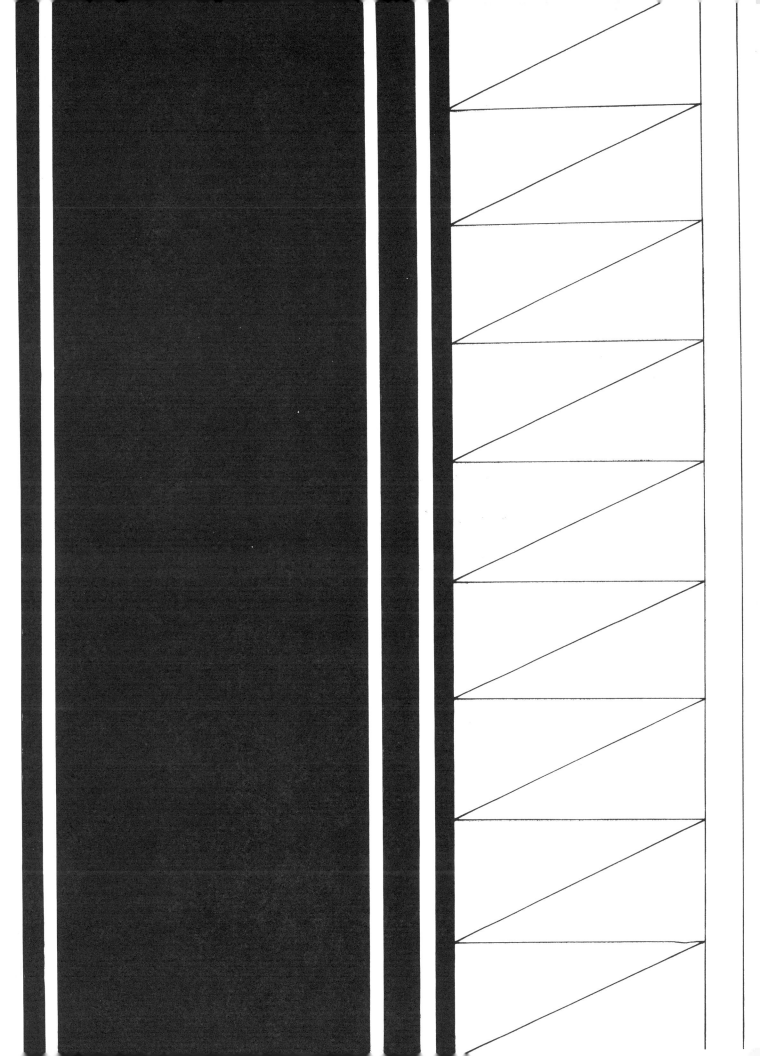

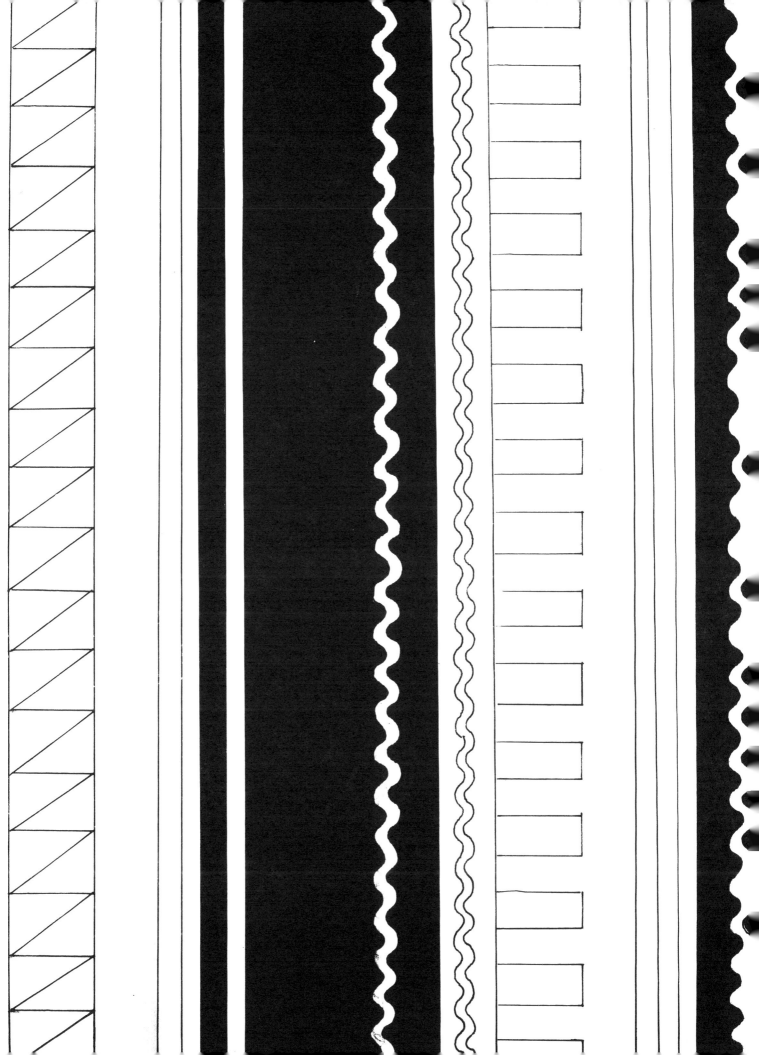

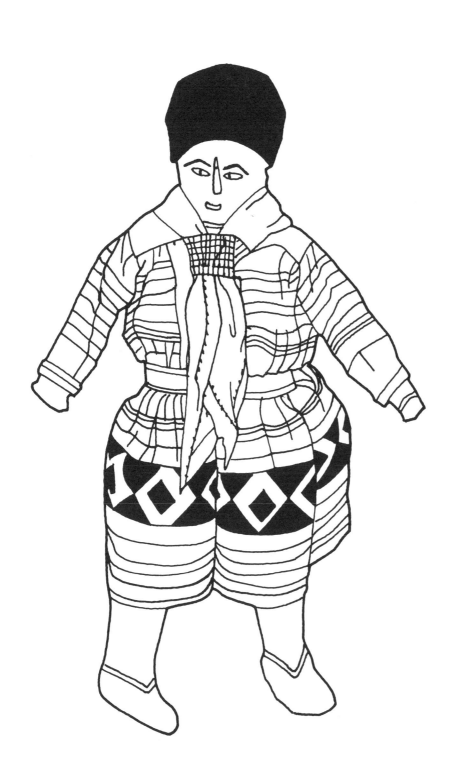

For Kaye Exo,
a true friend
and splendid example
in an age when
women are learning
to be whole people

Designed by Barbara Holdridge
Composed in Times Roman by Brown Composition,
   Baltimore, Maryland
Printed on 75-pound Williamsburg Offset and
   bound by Victor Graphics, Inc., Baltimore, Maryland
Cover color separation by Sun Crown, Washington, D.C.
Cover printed by Strine Printing Company, York,
   Pennsylvania